France

First published in Great Britain in 1998 by
Colin Baxter Photography Ltd
Grantown-on-Spey, Moray PH26 3NA

A CIP catalogue record for this book is available from the British Library

ISBN 1 900455 50 1

Printed in Hong Kong

Front Cover Photograph: Château de la Malartrie, La Roque-Gageac, Dordogne
Back Cover Photograph: Le Prunier, Périgord Blanc, Dordogne

FRANCE

COLIN BAXTER

Colin Baxter Photography, Grantown-on-Spey, Scotland

FRANCE

It is a combination of many quite ordinary things that produces the special feeling of just being in France. Doors, windows, shutters and roofs blend in distinctive architectural styles across the many diverse regions. Market towns bustle with atmosphere and colour, small villages hold a timeless calm, and restaurants throughout the country indulge in the joy of good food and fine wine.

Gastronomy is of course one of France's great strengths and it is wedded not only to a way of life but to the shaping of the landscape itself. There are over four hundred accredited wines produced in France, and large areas of the landscape are clothed with a fabric of vines in serried ranks; a mesh of crooked dark shapes in winter, overflowing with vibrant greens in spring and a glorious mass of oranges and reds during the autumn.

The landscape is wide and varied, and although plains cover much of the country, they are dissected by four great rivers and their tributaries; the Seine, Loire, Garonne and Rhône, as well as many other smaller rivers, producing a giant jigsaw of fertile valleys and gorges. France also has over three thousand kilometres of coastline and harvesting of the sea as well as the land contributes to a vast array of mouth-watering menus.

Snow is not uncommon in many regions, transforming the landscape into a less familiar guise, and often a heavy frost coats everything in the stillness of bright whites. It is amongst the snow-covered mountains of Europe's highest peaks on the border with Italy and Switzerland that the land contrasts dramatically with the plains to the north and west. Along France's southern border with Spain as well dramatic scenery dominates, with jagged peaks towering above the wooded slopes and lush pastures below. In the Massif Central, deep winding gorges have been carved for thousands of years amongst long extinct volcanos. The soil is rich and along with the crops, sheep and cows it supports, there are large tracts of natural woodland cloaking the slopes alongside deep meandering rivers. A quarter of France is in fact forest and in places still harbours wildlife species otherwise very rare in Western Europe.

It is however the history of France that has shaped the character of the landscape more than anything, and its legacy is everywhere. Monuments to the French Revolution abound, great Renaissance chateaux dominate their surroundings; Gothic architecture stands proud in towns and cities; the countryside overflows with a wealth of beautiful Romanesque churches; Medieval towns are remarkably intact; and in the south, impressive Roman structures have survived two thousand years of wars and weather.

France's unique blend of history and landscape is also transformed by the seasons, producing more than a lifetime of situations to experience, explore and indeed to capture with a camera. The photographs here are a selection of such places and moments across the country's differing regions. They are a personal collection gleaned from travels over many years and very much an indulgence in rural France, in the landscape, its towns, villages and buildings, from the humble to the grandiose. There is of course much more to explore and I will certainly, in the years to come, continue to enjoy discovering the visual delights France has to behold.

Colin Baxter

Bonaguil, Lot *(opposite)*

Mont Blanc, Haute-Savoie

Ingersheim, Alsace

Cingle de Montfort, Dordogne

Vergt, Dordogne

Sorède, Roussillon

Najac, Gorges de l'Aveyron

Apetchia, Pays Basque

Saint-Michel, Pays Basque

Moulès-et-Baucels, Hérault

Périgord Noir

15

Ribérac, Périgord Blanc *(left)*
Le Moulin de Puy d'Ardanne, Vienne *(opposite)*

Journans, Ain

Cirque de Navacelles, Languedoc

Cingle de Trémolat, Dordogne

Côte Vermeille, Pyrénées-Orientales

Castillon-la-Bataille, Gironde

22

Château de la Malartrie, La Roque-Gageac, Dordogne

Gorges de la Dourbie, Cévennes

Prunet-et-Belpuig, Pyrénées-Orientales

25

Haut-Rhin, Alsace

Izeron, Isère

27

Dune du Pilat, Gironde

28

Pays de la Loire

Périgord Blanc

Le Prunier, Périgord Blanc

Pas-de-Calais

Normandie

Chambord, Loir-et-Cher

34

Castelnaud-la-Chapelle, Dordogne

Saint Emilion, Gironde

Causse Bégon, Cévennes

Chaîne des Albères, Pyrénées-Orientales

Collioure, Côte Vermeille, Pyrénées-Orientales

39

La Chambon, Saône-et-Loire

Arcy, Saône-et-Loire

Ribeauvillé, Alsace

Riquewihr, Alsace

43

Plan-des-Berthats, Haute-Savoie

Marlens, Haute-Savoie

Salers, Cantal, Auvergne

46

Cantal, Auvergne

Amphoux, Provence

Le Cher, Indre-et-Loire

49

Rhône

La Bourbince, Paray-le-Monial, Saône-et-Loire

Sainte Colome, Pyrénées-Atlantique

Pau, Pyrénées-Atlantique

Var, Provence

La Camargue, Bouches-du-Rhône

Rochefort-sur-Loire, Pays de la Loire

Dole, Jura

Rochers de Monges, Quercy *(opposite)*
Amiens, Picardie *(right)*

Périgueux, Dordogne

Cannes, Côte d'Azur

Argensac, Périgord Blanc

Chenonceaux, Indre-et-Loire

63

Saint Vincent-de-Connezac, Dordogne

Clécy, La Suisse Normande, Calvados

La Saône, Mâcon, Bourgogne

La Roche, Bourgogne

Périgord Blanc

68

Périgord Blanc

Berre-des-Alpes, Alpes-Maritimes

Moroges, Bourgogne

71

Saint Malo, Bretagne

Saumur, Pays de la Loire

Gorges du Tarn, Lozère

Peyre Martine, Hérault

La Grande Clavelie, Périgord Blanc

76

Côte Vermeille, Pyrénées-Orientales

77

Châteaudun, Eure-et-Loir

Oberhaslach, Alsace

Roussillon *(above)*
Le Mont-Saint-Michel, Basse-Normandie *(opposite)*

Antibes, Côte d'Azur *(opposite)*
Saussignac, Dordogne *(above)*

83

Puig de las Daynes, Pyrénées-Orientales

Palalda, Pyrénées-Orientales

Ambonnay, Champagne

Périgord Blanc

Servance, Haute-Saône

Ballon de Servance, Haute-Saône

Le Tronchet, Basse-Normandie

Saint-Julien-de-la-Nef, Gard

Les Aspres, Pyrénées-Orientales

Nadaillac-de-Rouge, Quercy

Montmelard, Bourgogne

94

L'Escarène, Alpes-Maritimes

Barjols, Provence

Gorges de la Vis, Languedoc

Chaîne des Aravis, Haute-Savoie

Manigod, Haute-Savoie

Château de la Treyne, Quercy

Villandry, Indre-et-Loire

Port-Vendres, Pyrénées-Orientales

Soutayrol, Languedoc

Pointe du Raz, Bretagne

Poulgoazec, Bretagne

Beynac-et-Cazenac, Dordogne

Monpazier, Dordogne

Pont du Gard, Languedoc

Hautefort, Périgord Vert

Pontevès, Provence *(left)*
Rocamadour, Lot *(opposite)*

INDEX OF PLACES